Adult Coloring book Dragons & Castles

Vol 4

By: L. M. Boelz

I want to take a moment to thank you for purchasing this coloring book.

A lot of time went into the making of it. I wanted to be able to give you hours of fun

and relaxation. So Enjoy. Be sure to check out my other coloring books if you

like this one.   There are 20 different pictures to color in this book.

Other titles

Chickens Vol. 1

Southwest, Floral Vol 2

Day of the Dead & Madri Gras Vol 3

Farm Animals Vol 5

pages

Fire in the Sky.. 1
Guardian...... 2
Floating Castle... 3
Zargafar.. 4
Serpent........ 5
Dragon On a Pillar...................................... 6
Dragon Pit... 7
Castle Moat.. 8
Castle Shrooms.. 9
Dragon on a Pedestal................................... 10
Dragon Lagoon 11
Dragon Fire... 12
Castle Bridge... 13
Filigree Dragon... 14
Castle Lake... 15
Castle Spire with Dragon............................... 16
Flaming Dragon.. 17
Cave Dragon 18
Water Dragon 19
Castle Courtyard 20

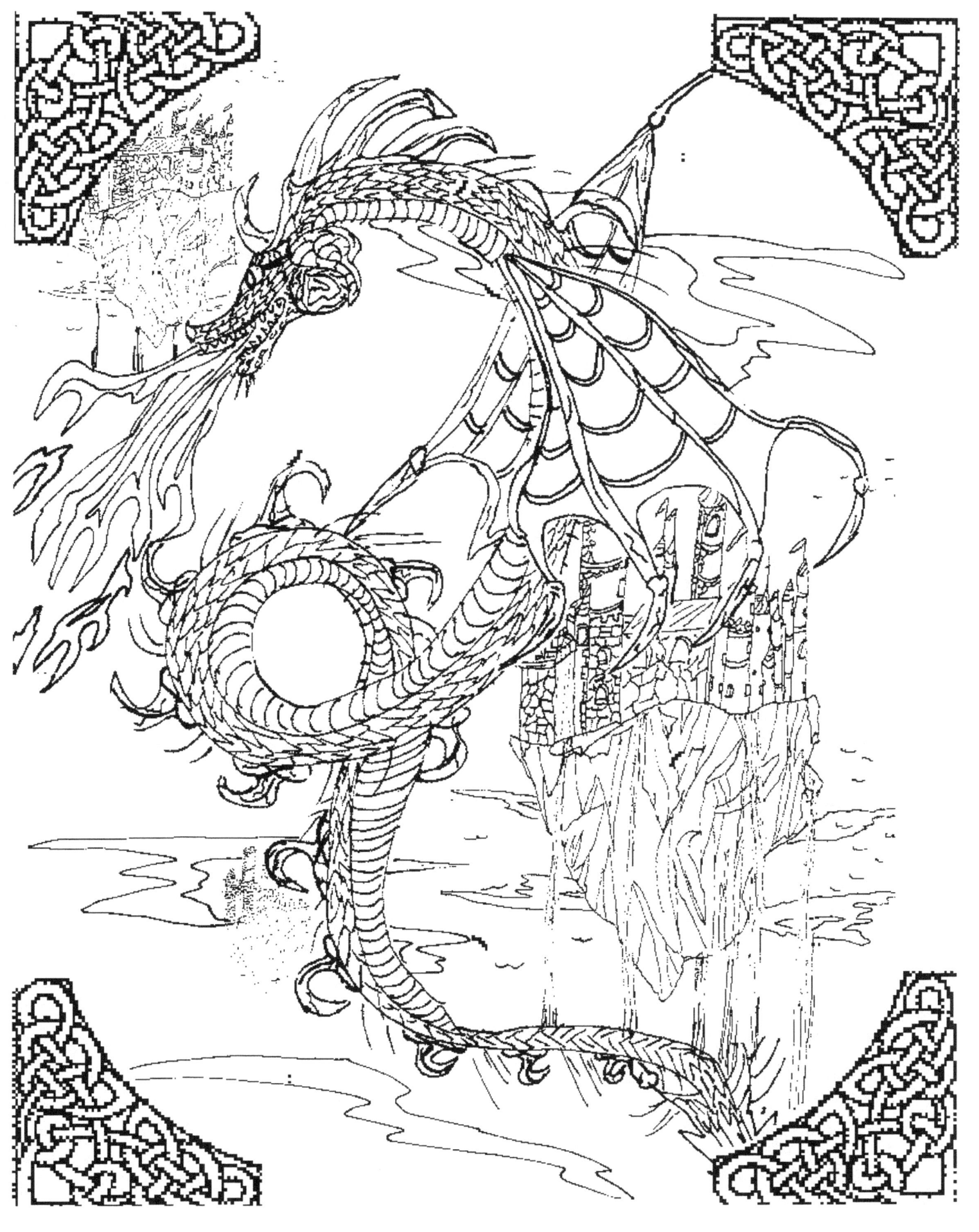

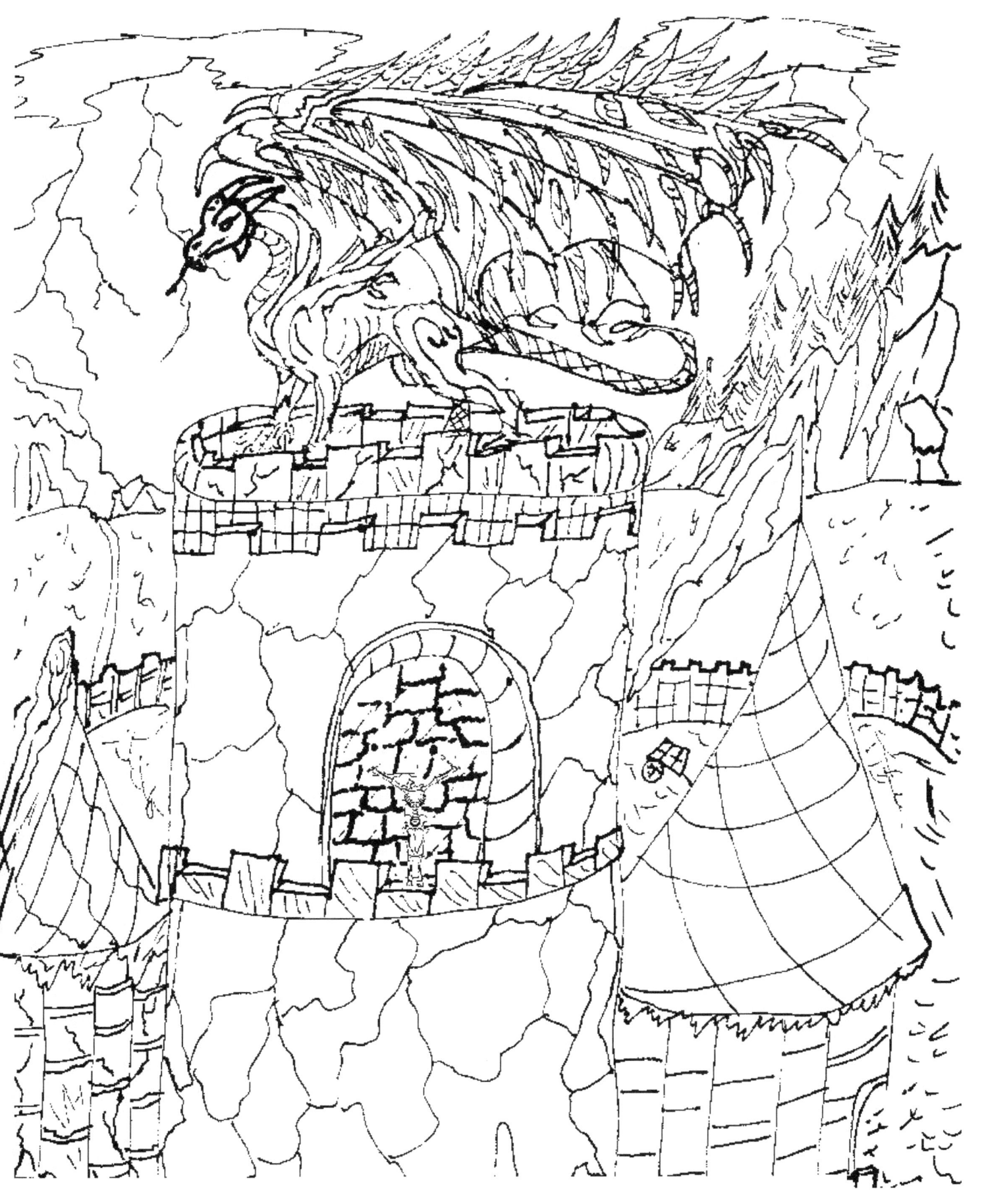

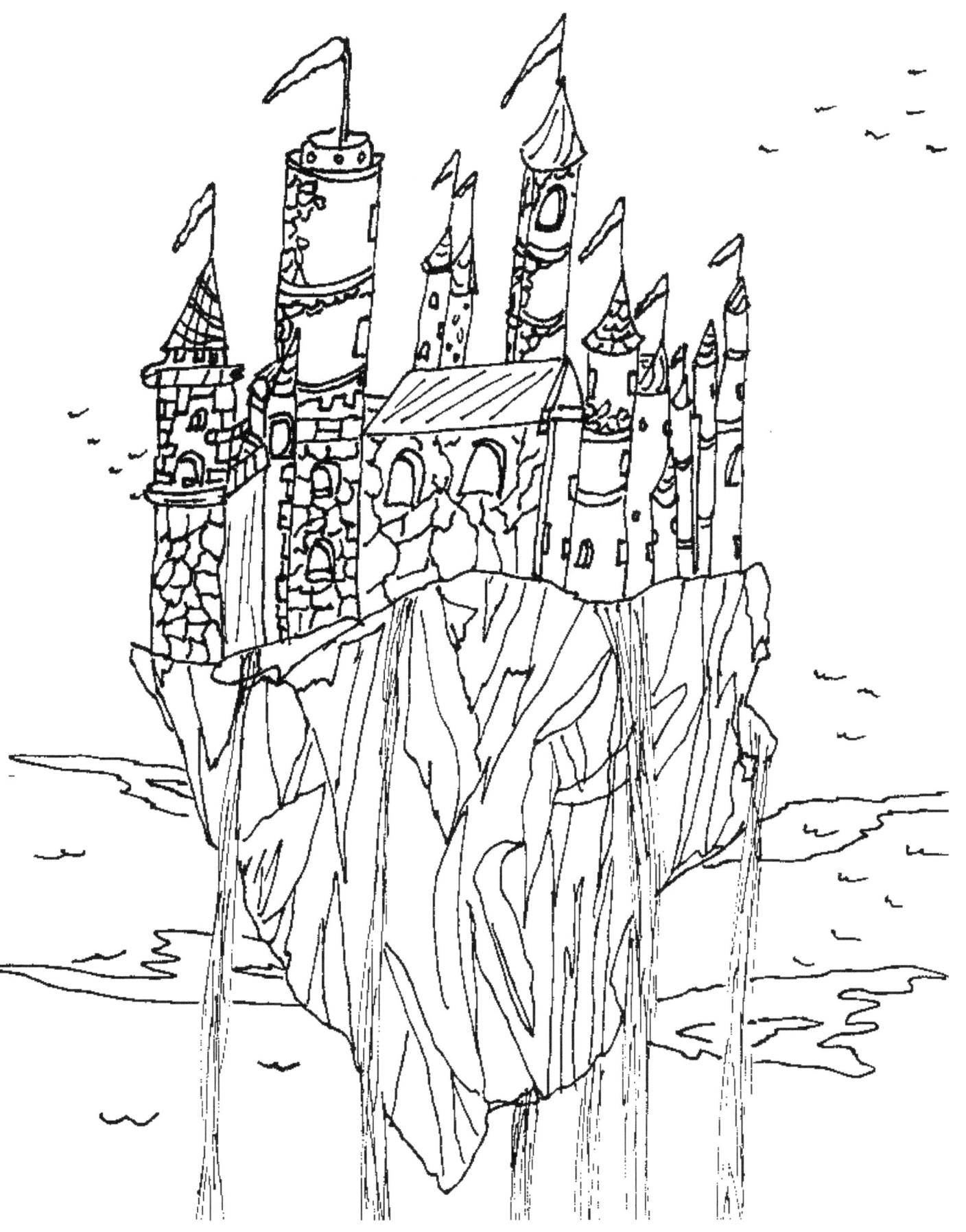

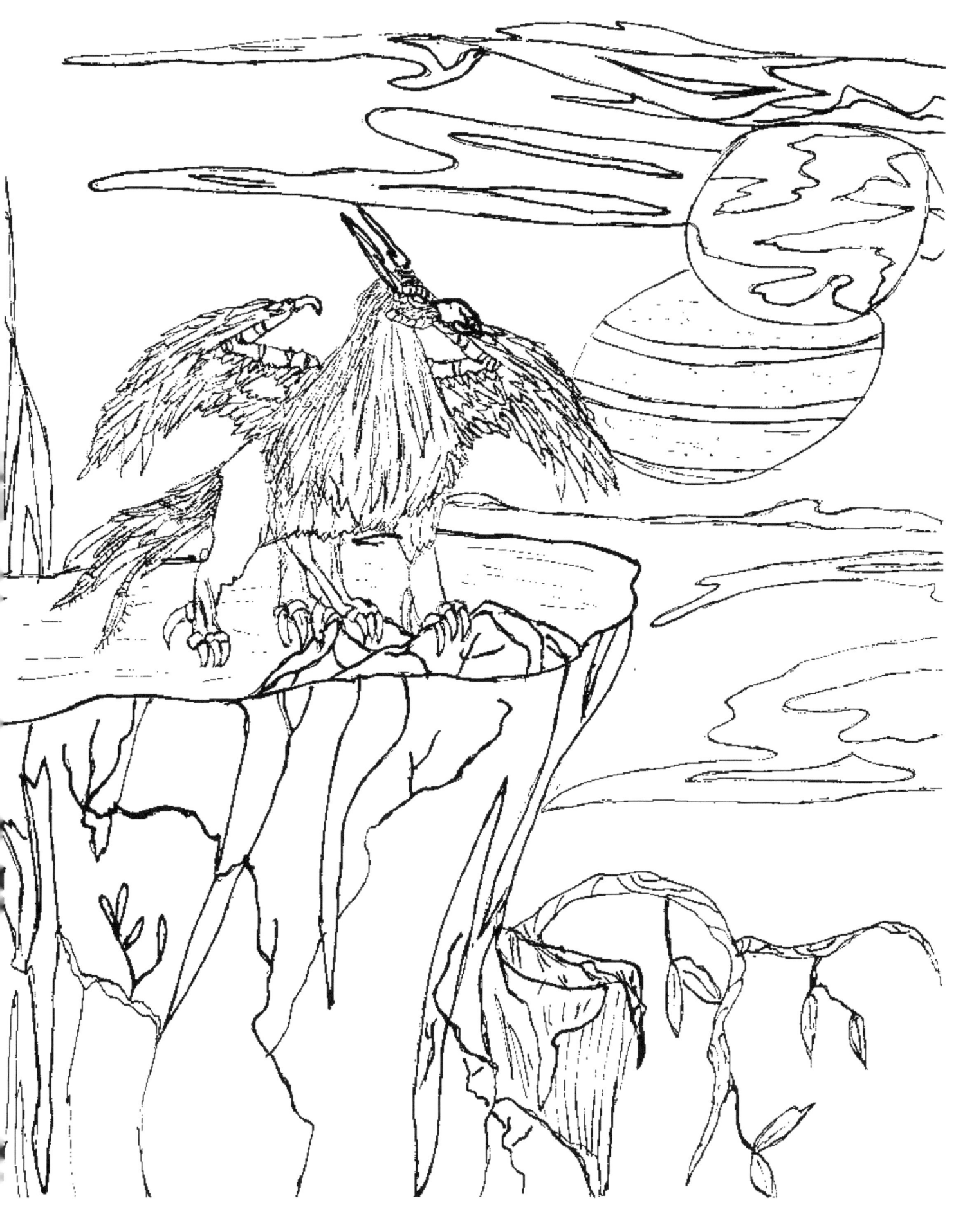

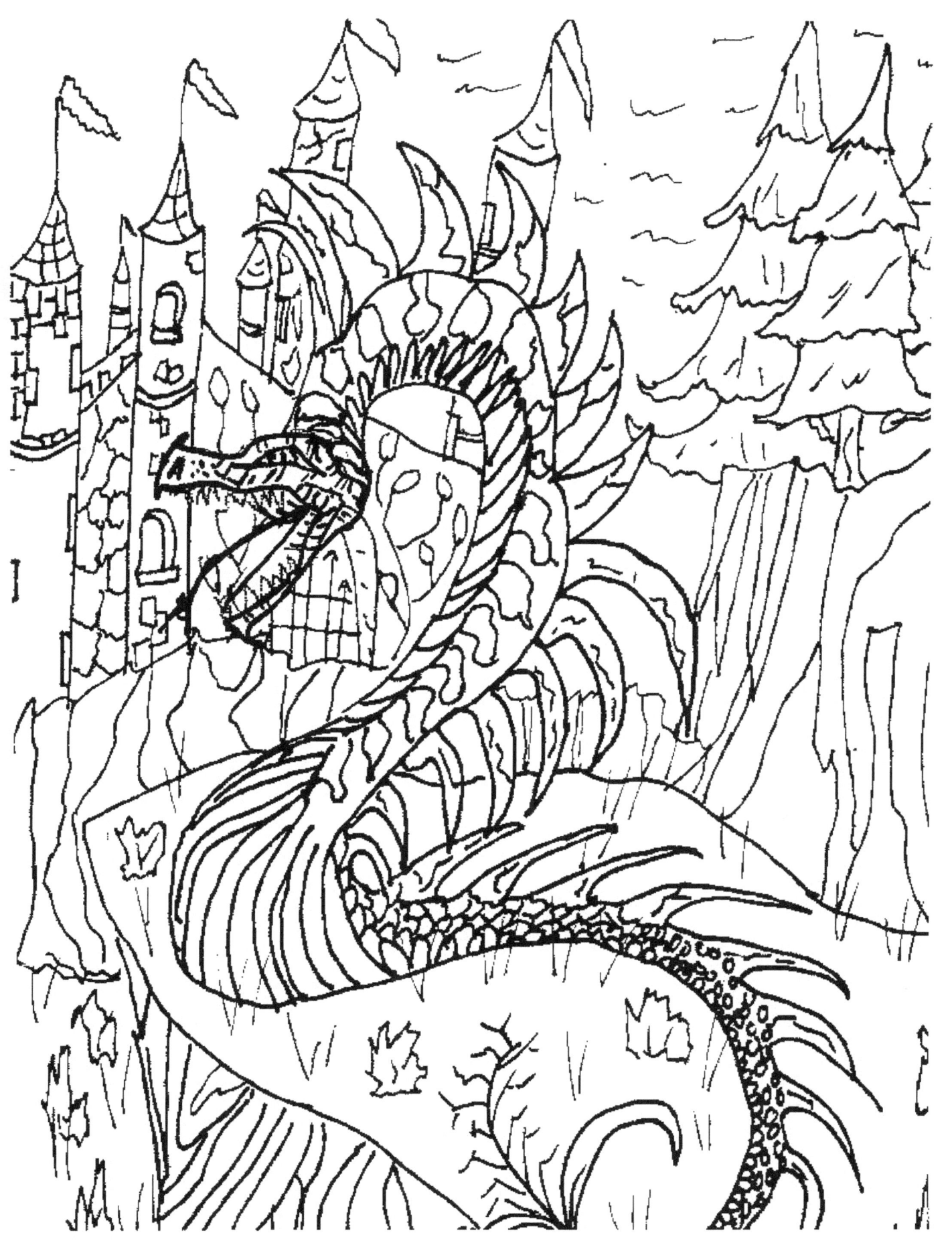

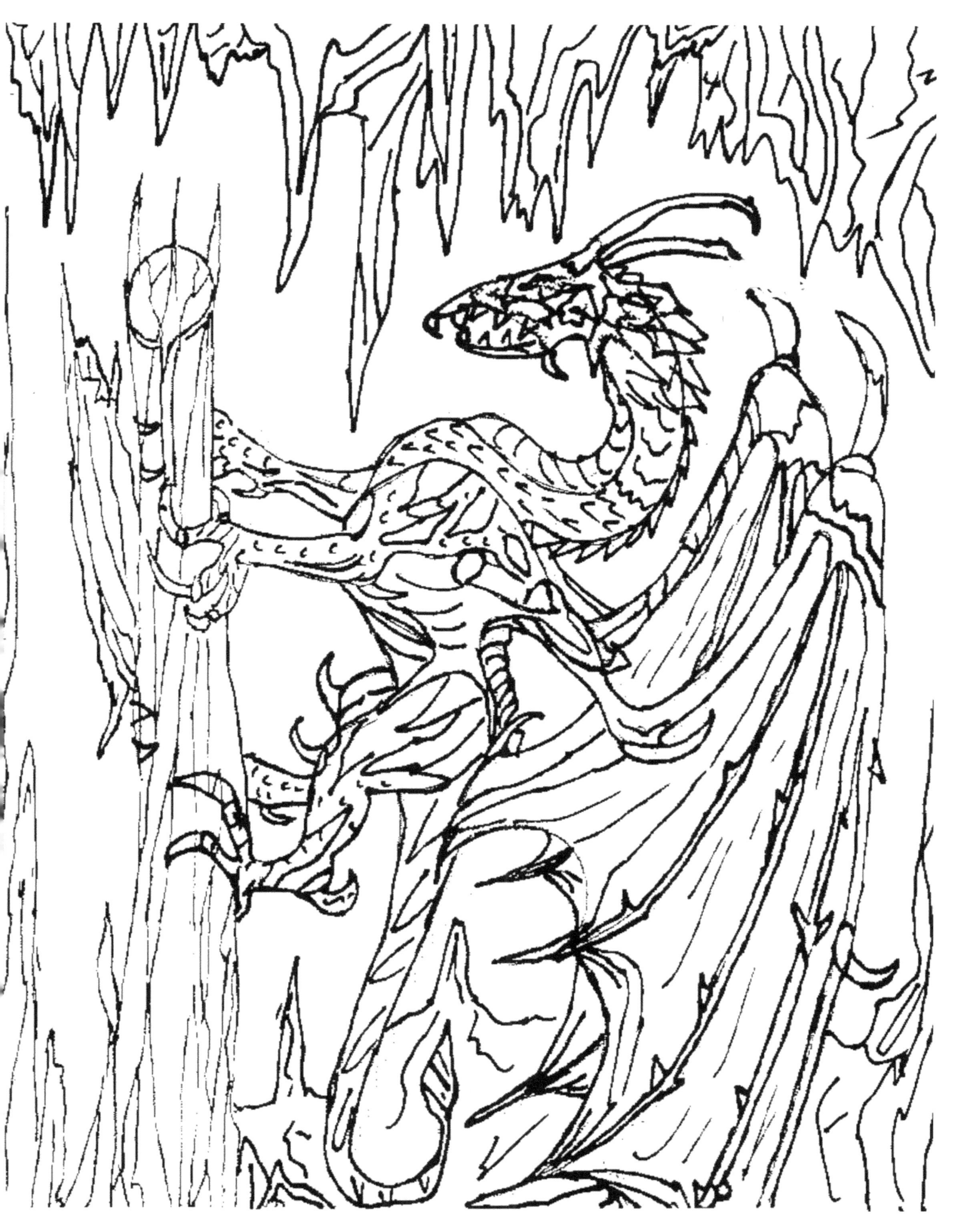

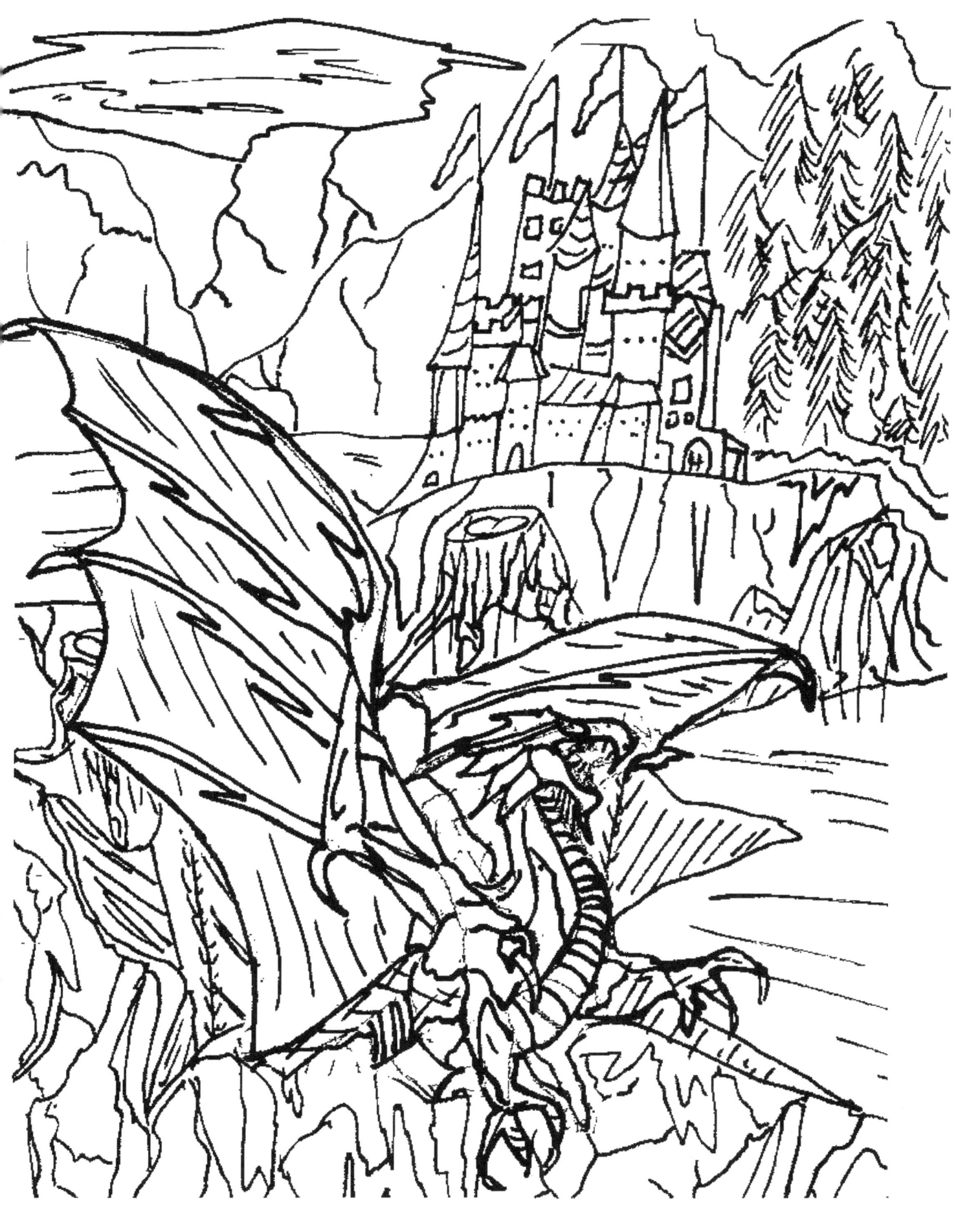

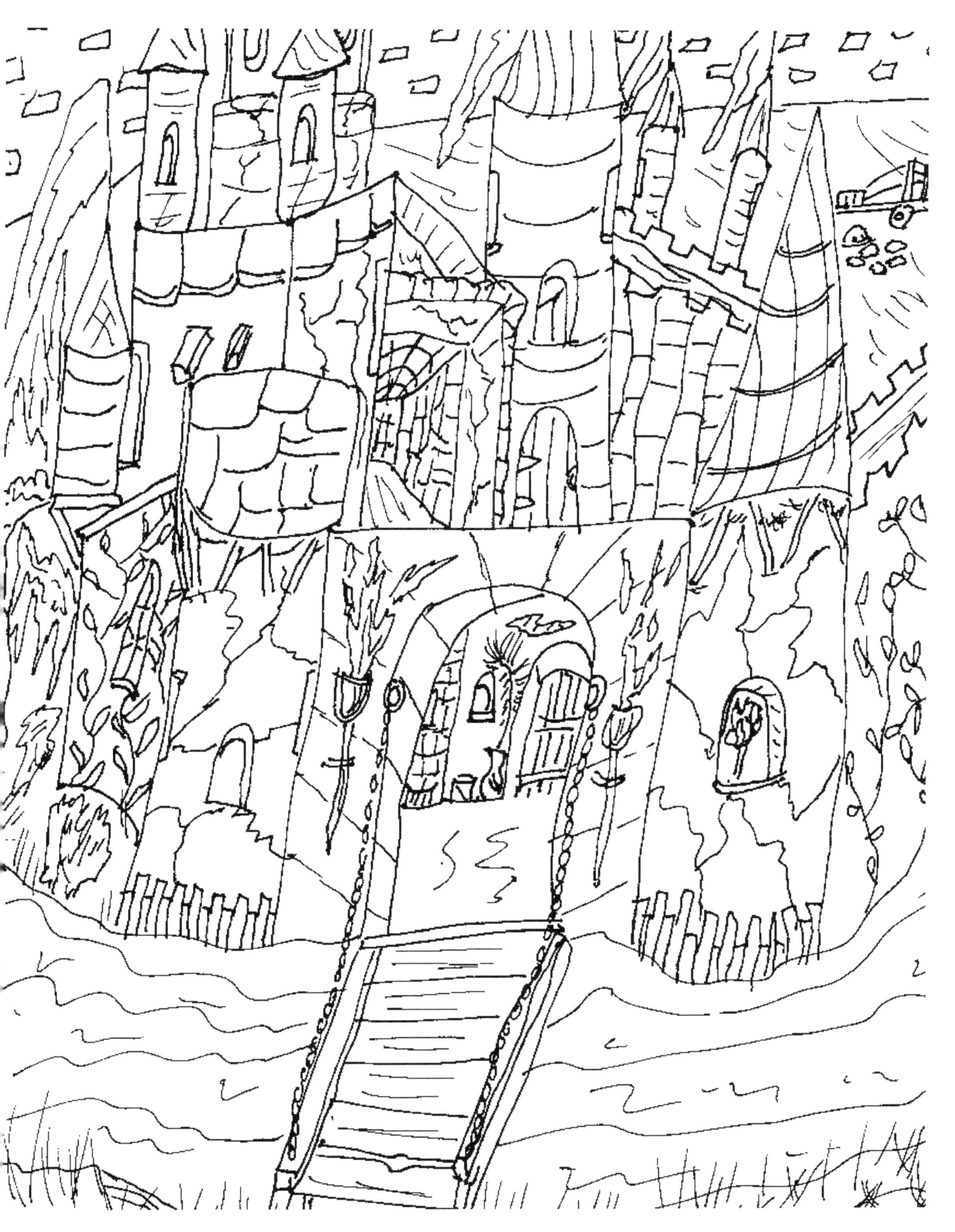

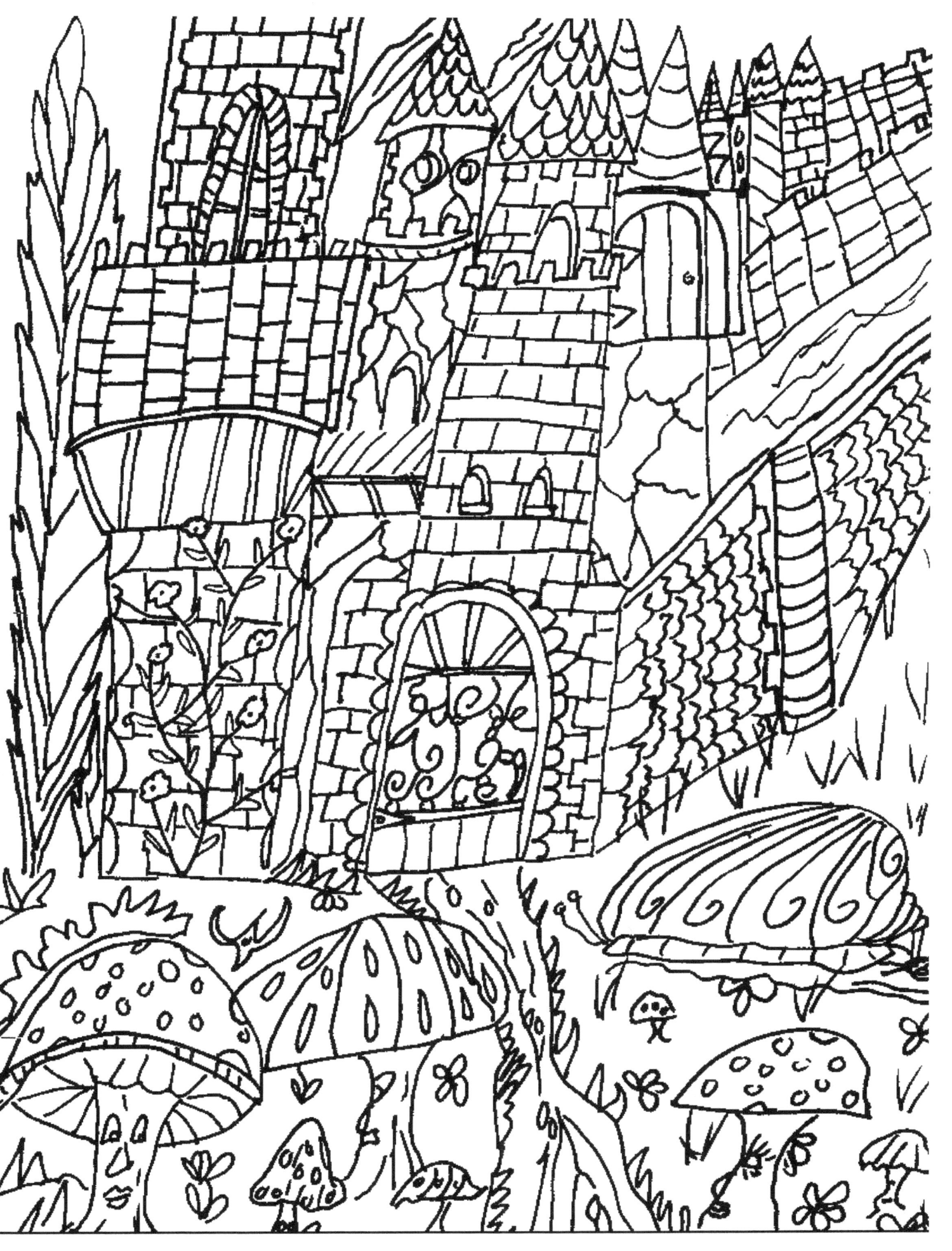

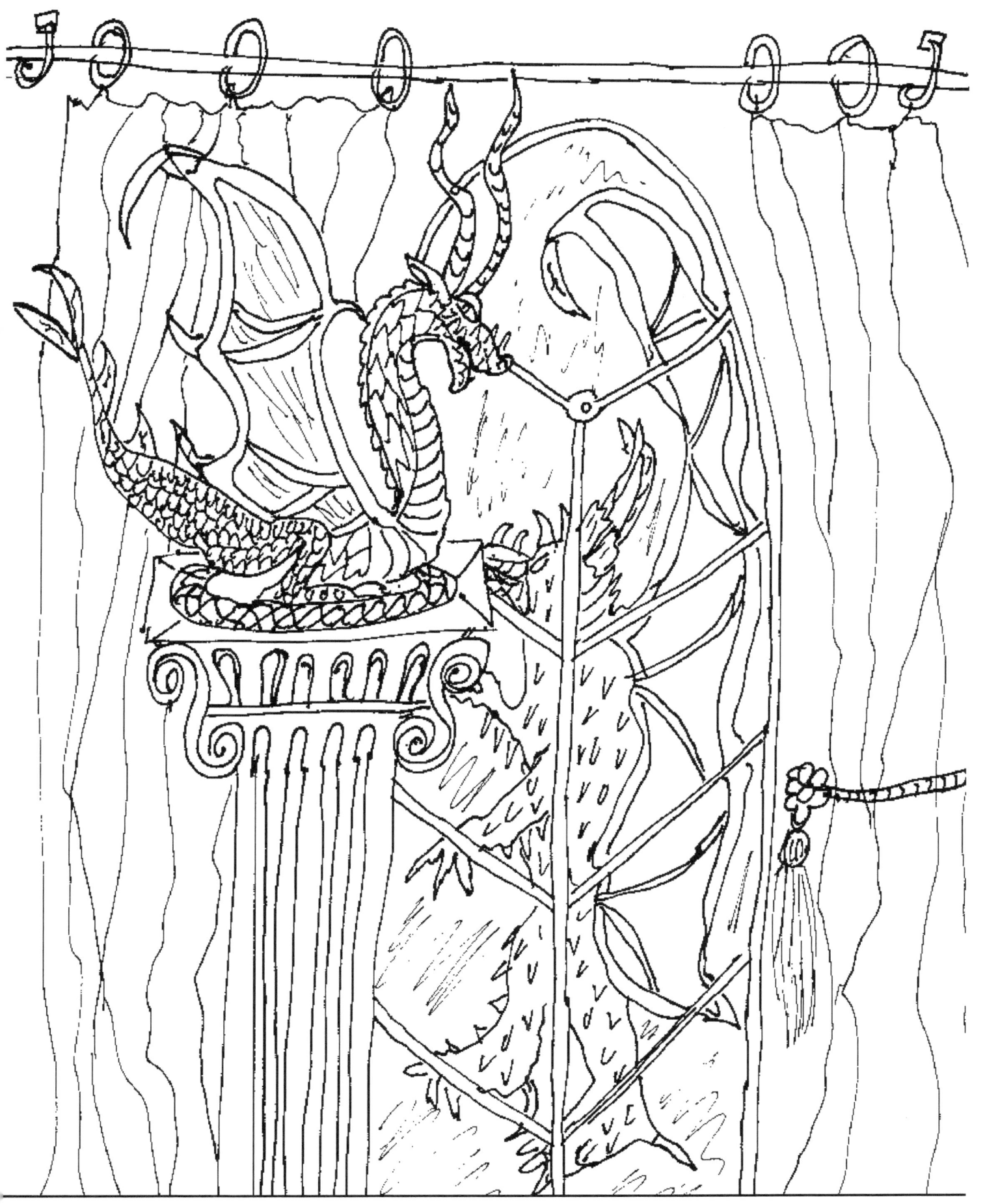

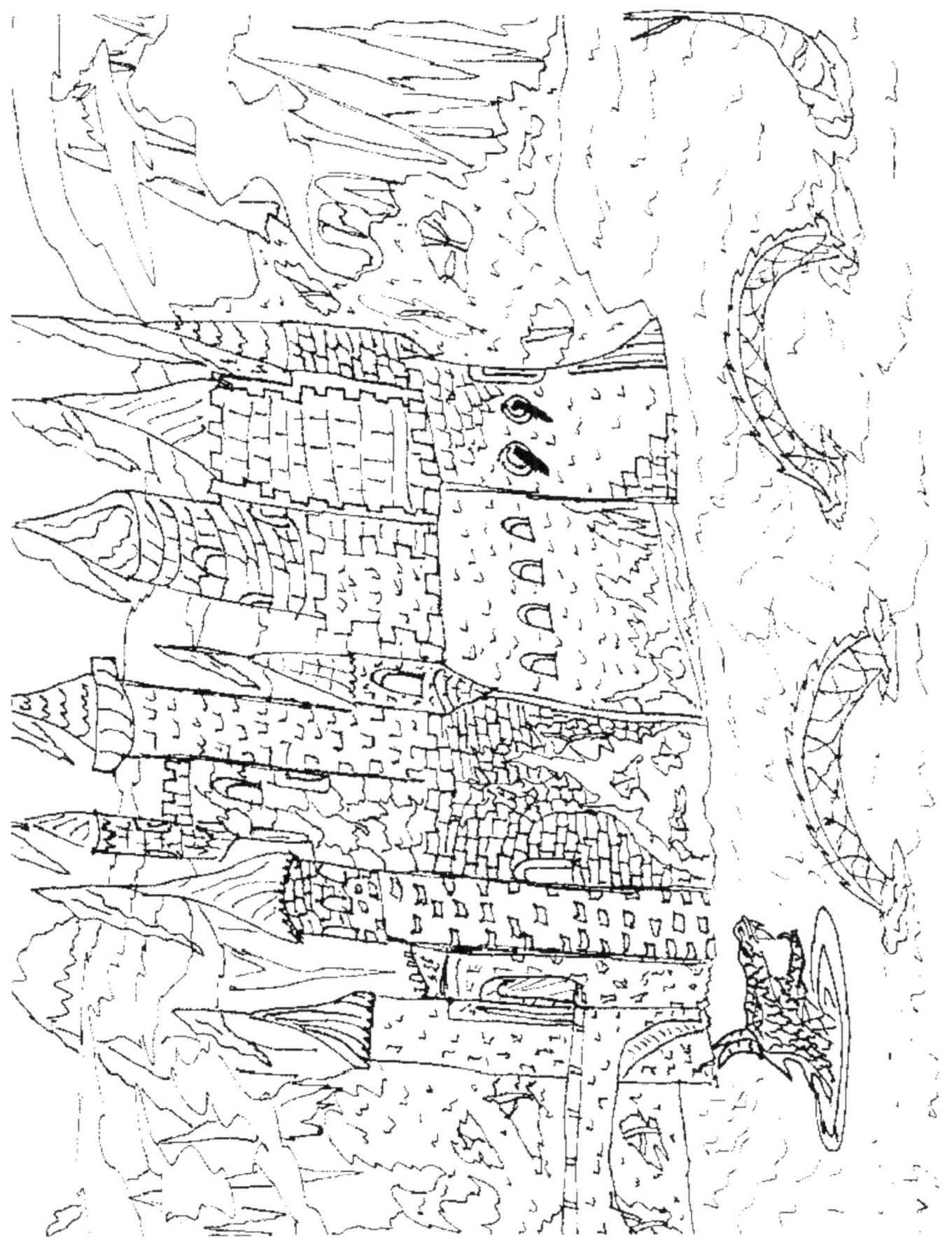

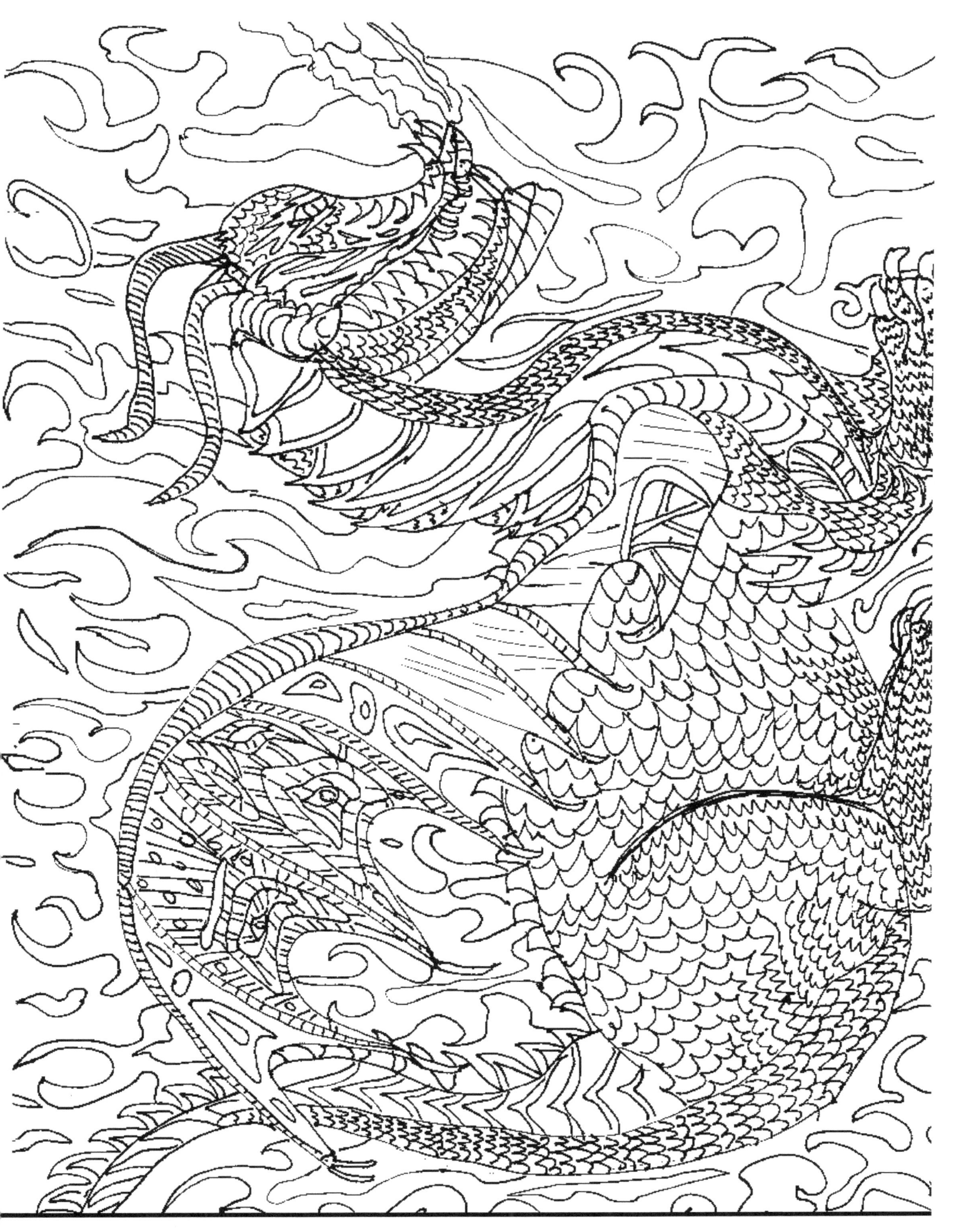

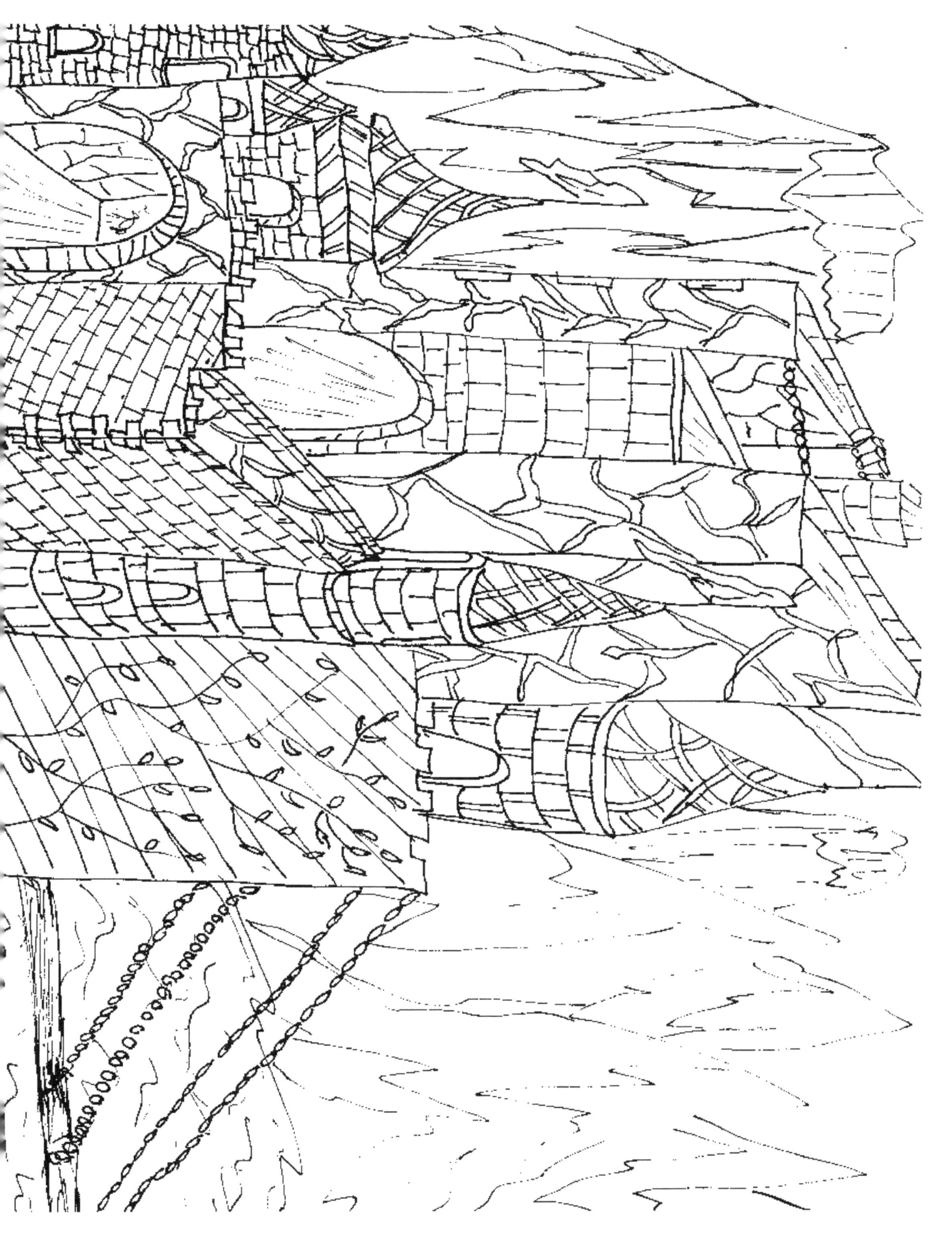

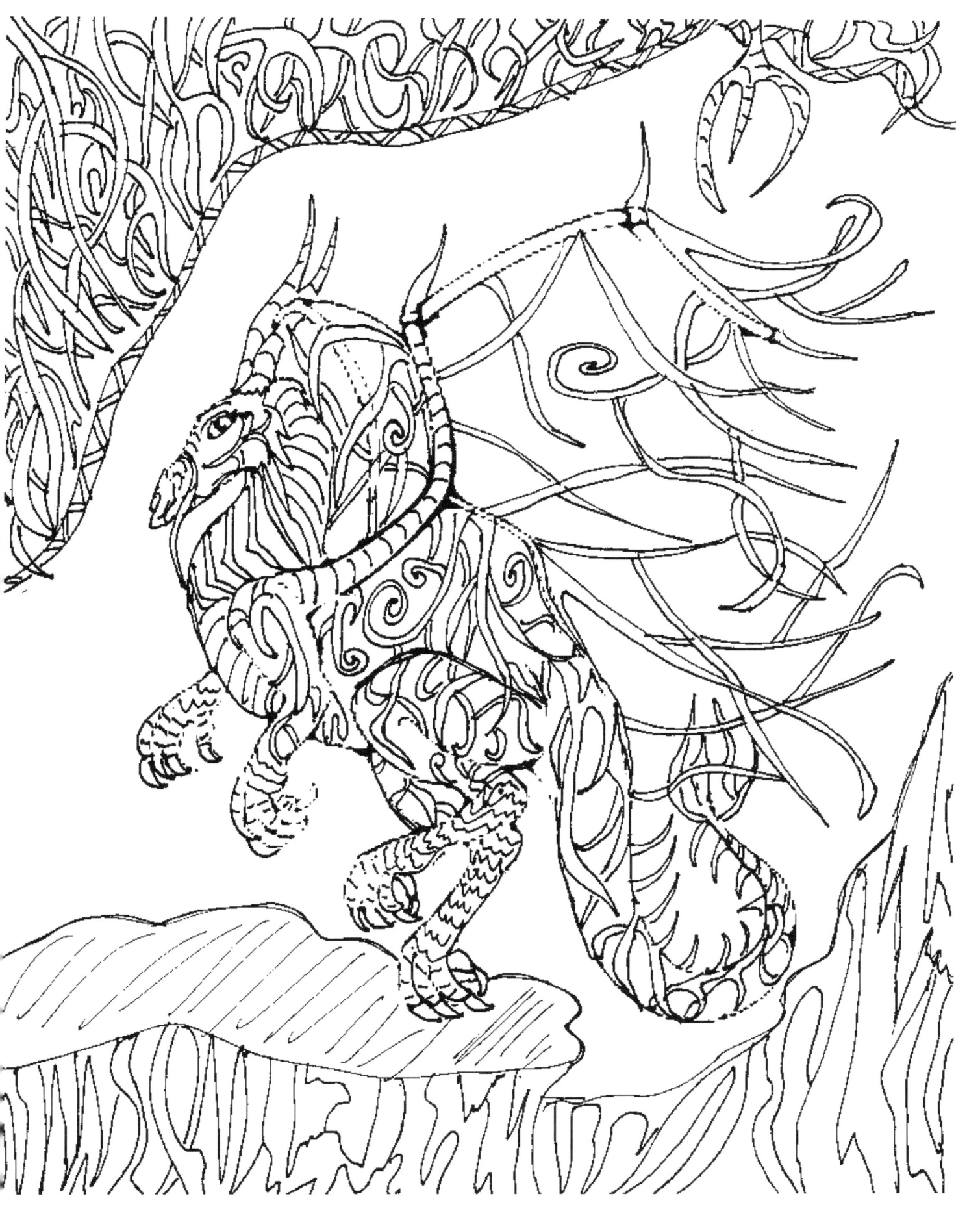

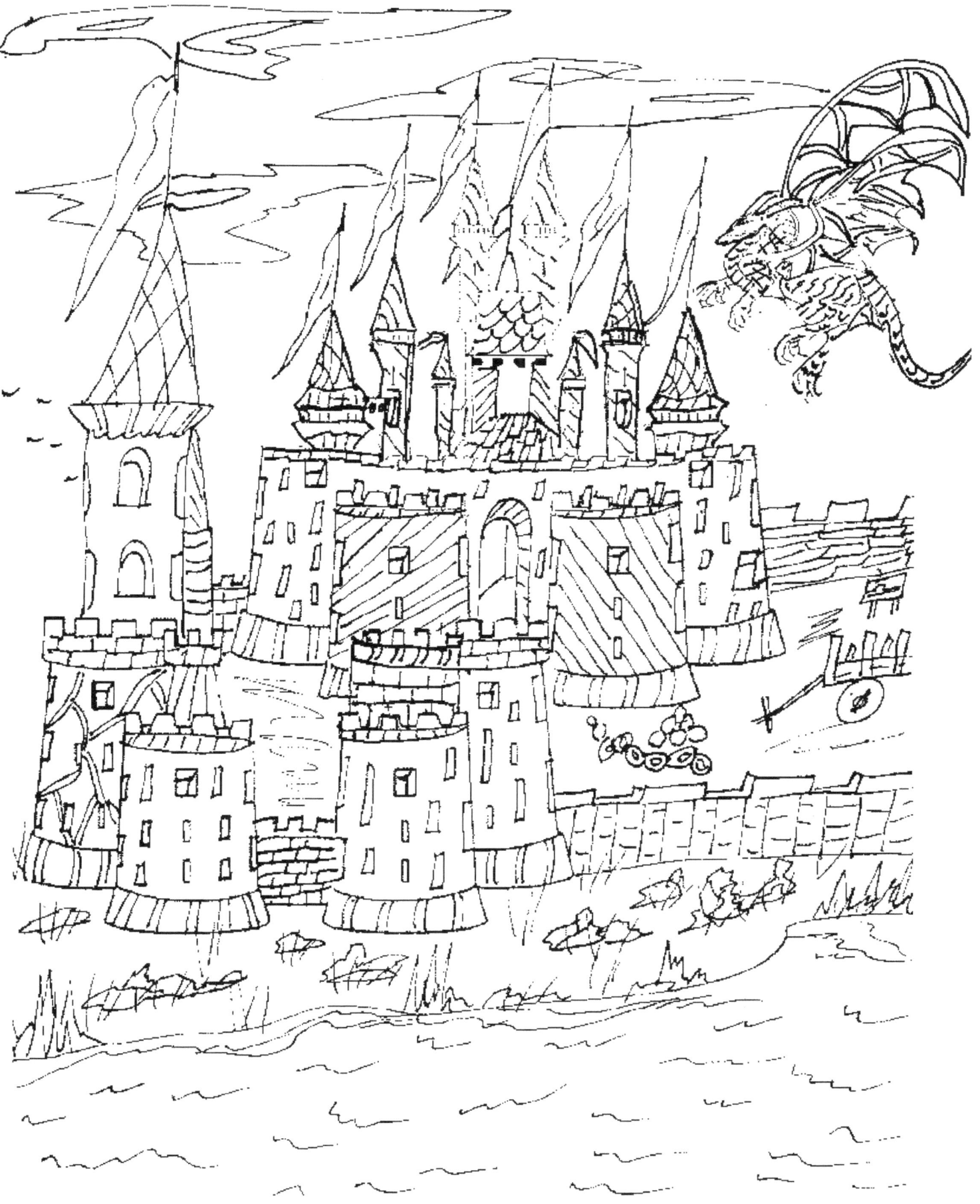

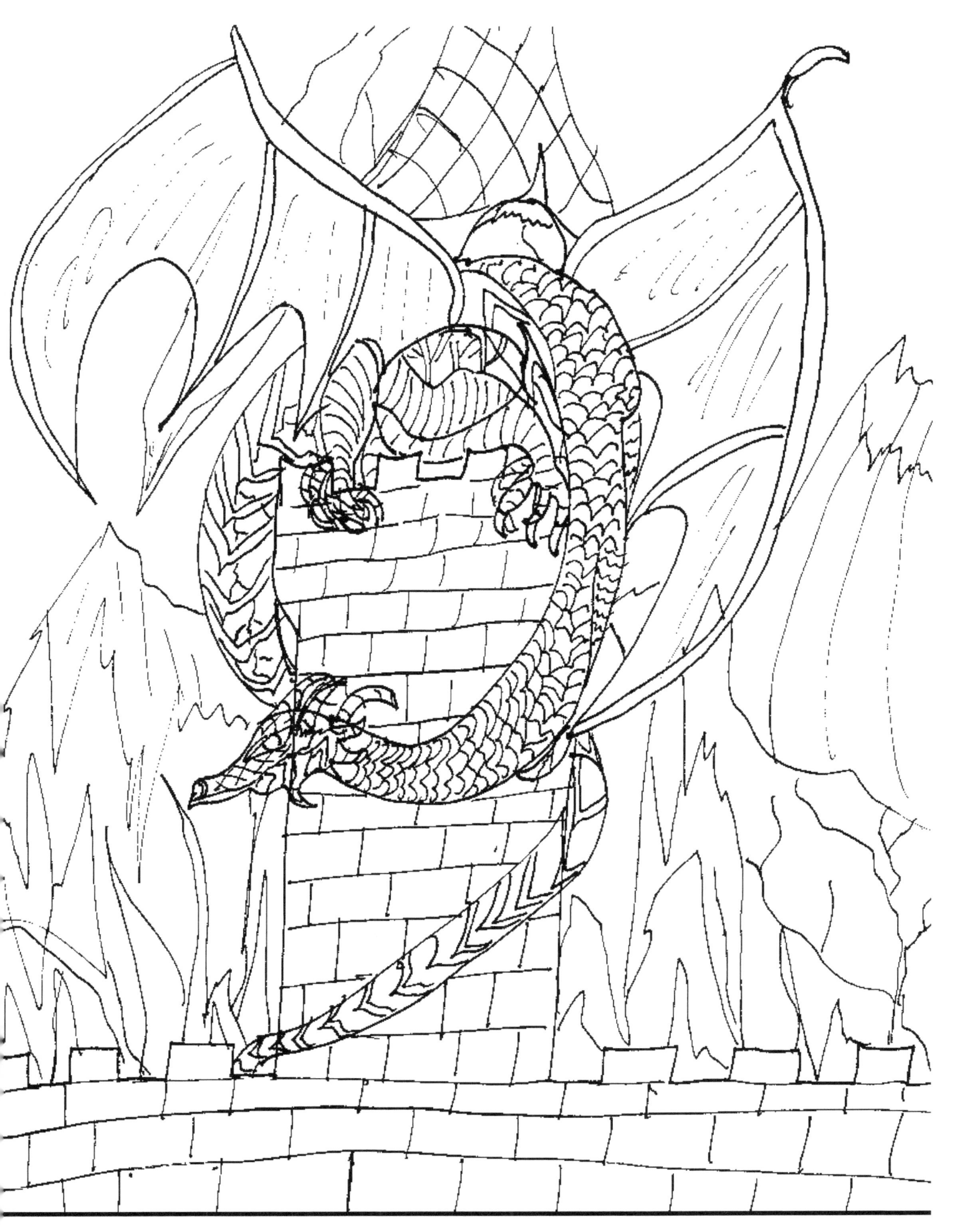

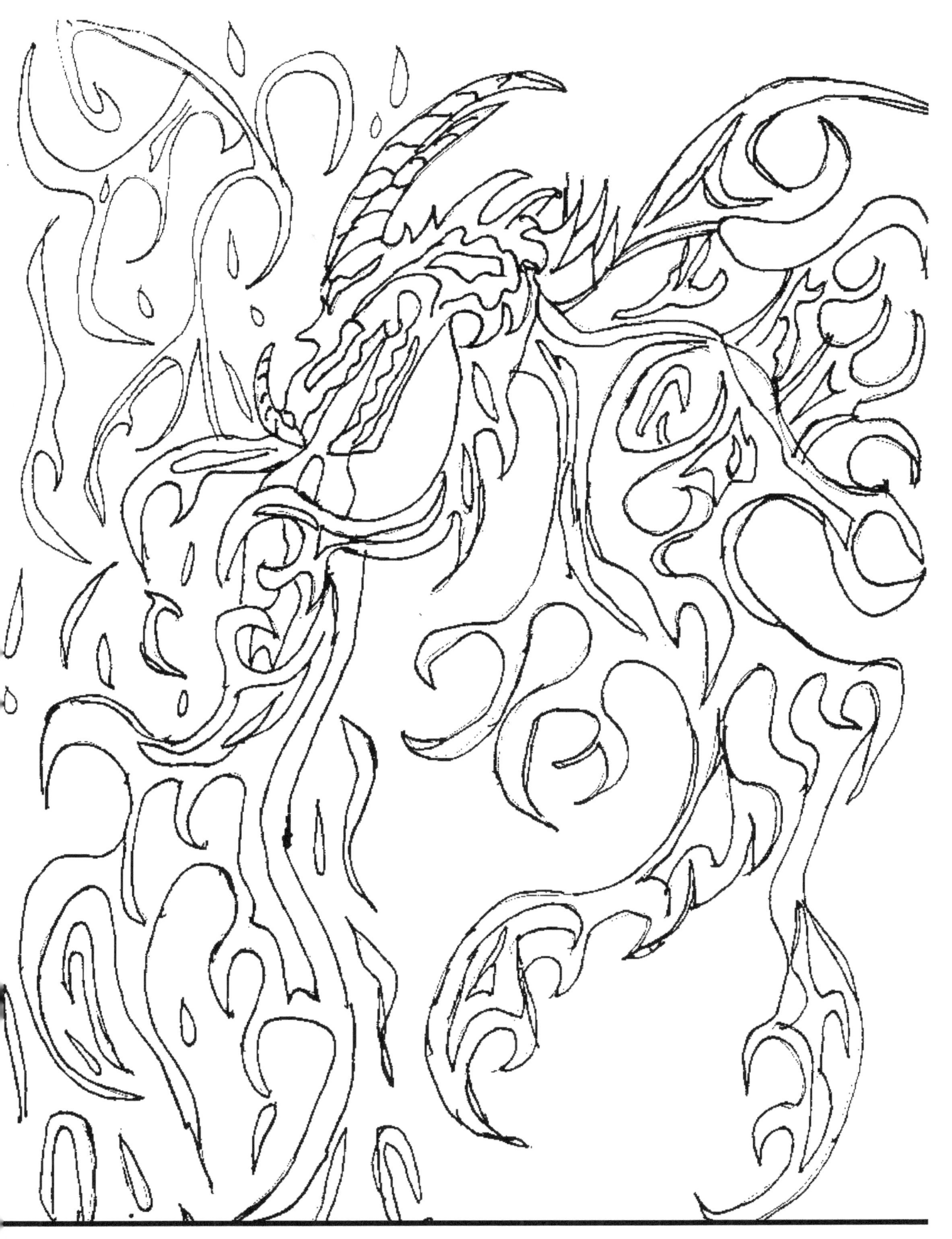

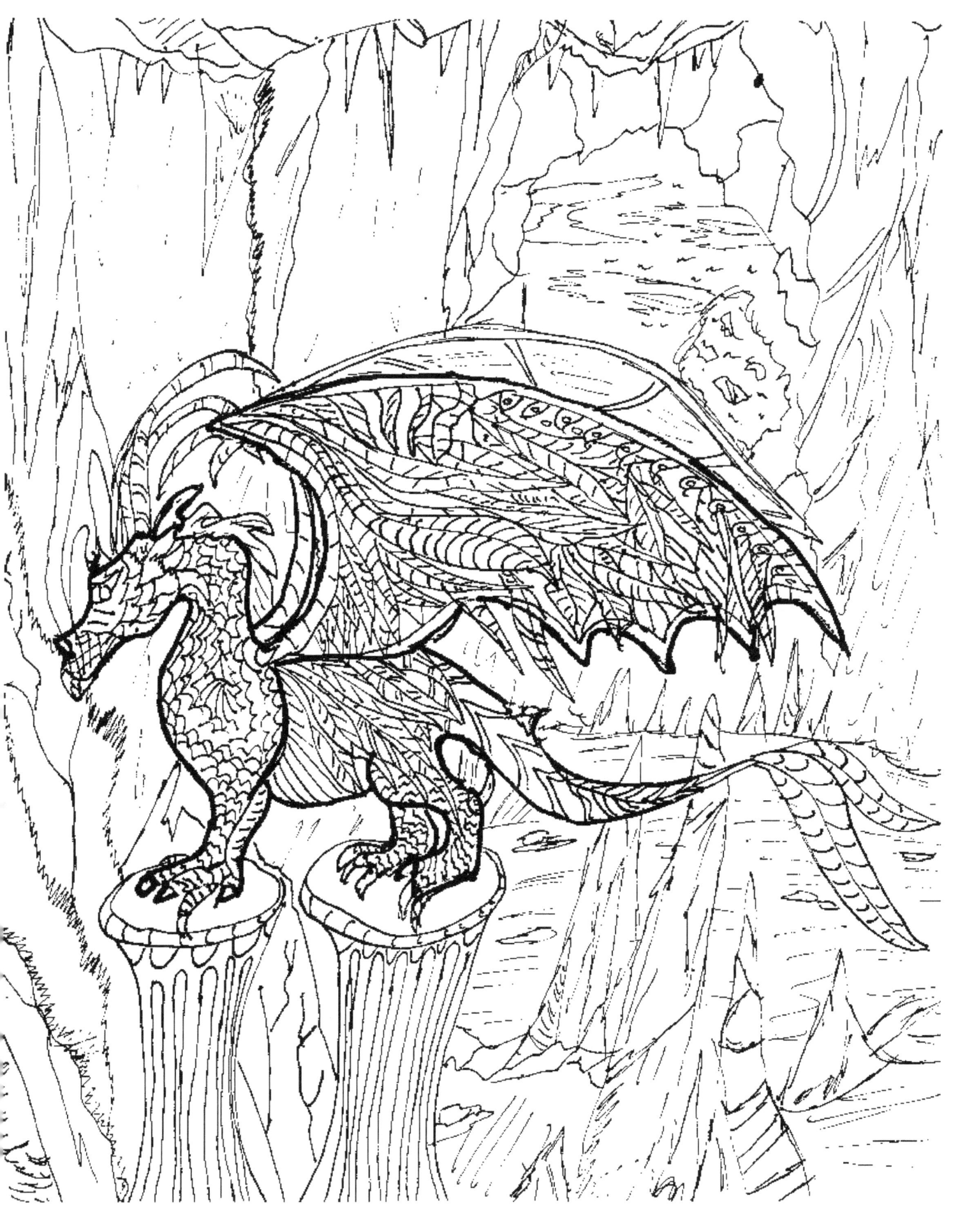

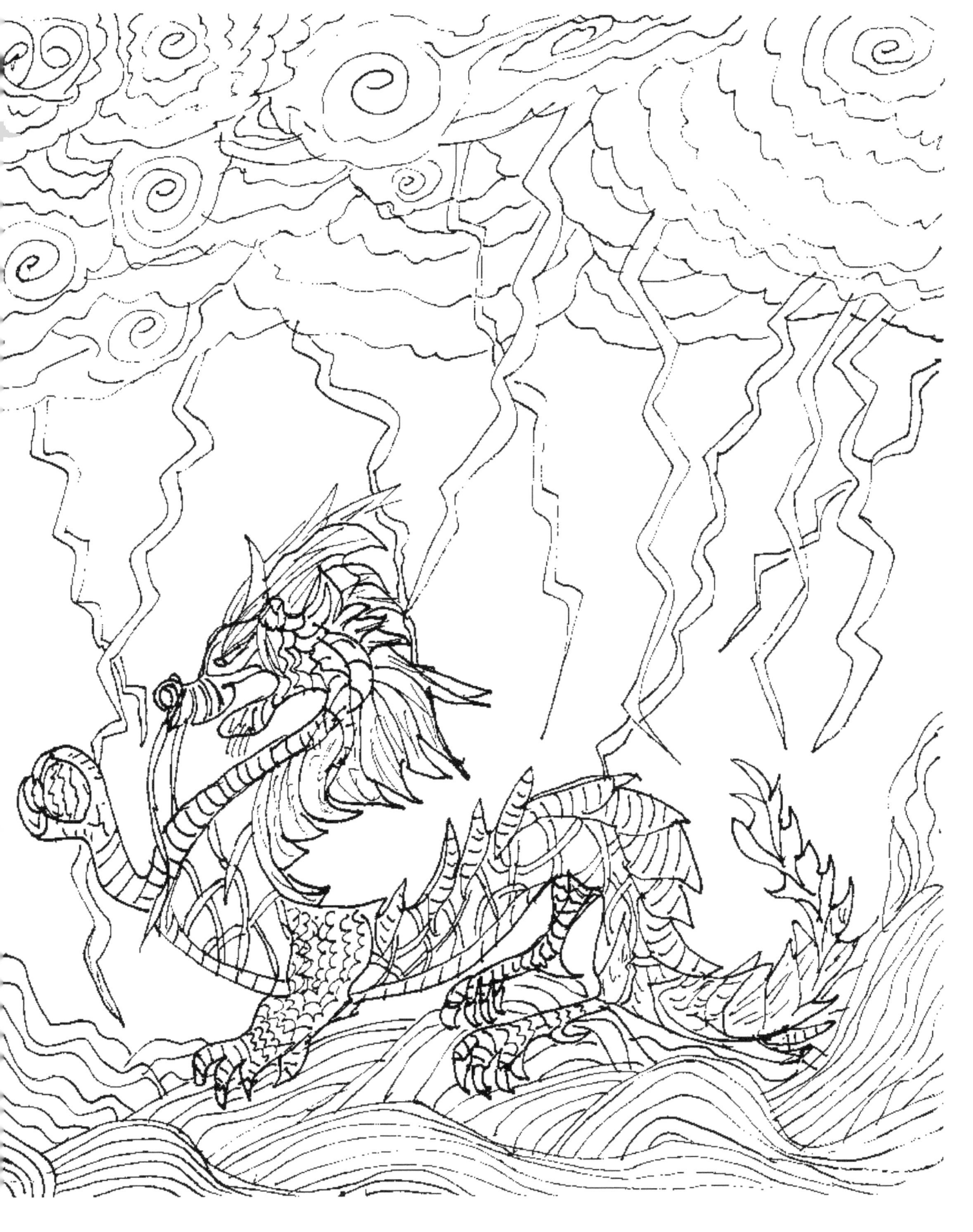

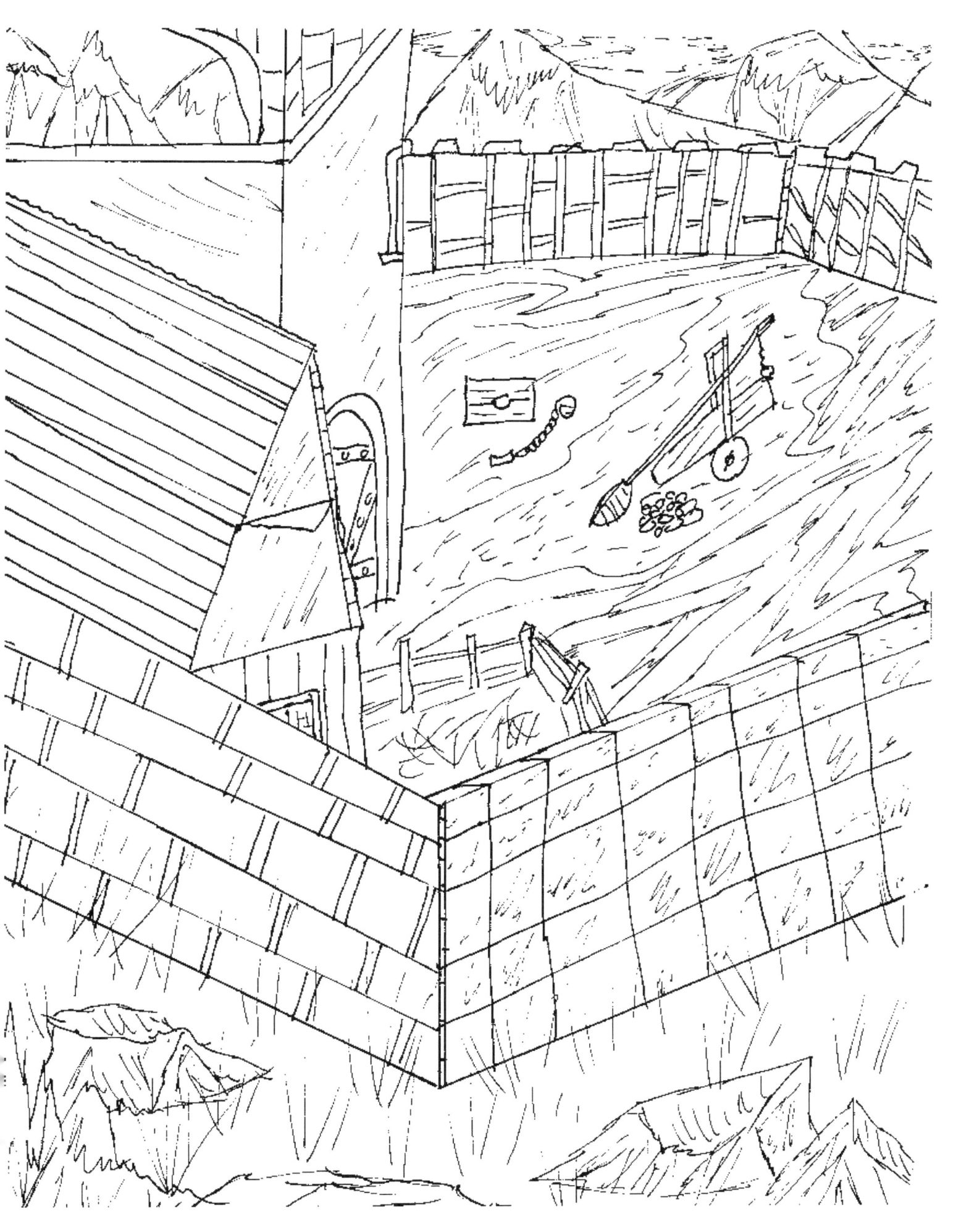